Recycling

Glass

Kate Walker

 **Marshall Cavendish**
Benchmark
New York

This edition first published in 2011 in the United States of America by
Marshall Cavendish Benchmark
An imprint of Marshall Cavendish Corporation

Website: www.marshallcavendish.us

This publication represents the opinions and views of the author based on Kate Walker's personal experience, knowledge, and research. The information in this book serves as a general guide only. The author and publisher have used their best efforts in preparing this book and disclaim liability rising directly and indirectly from the use and application of this book.

Other Marshall Cavendish Offices:
Marshall Cavendish International (Asia) Private Limited, 1 New Industrial Road, Singapore 536196 • Marshall Cavendish International (Thailand) Co Ltd. 253 Asoke, 12th Flr, Sukhumvit 21 Road, Klongtoey Nua, Wattana, Bangkok 10110, Thailand • Marshall Cavendish (Malaysia) Sdn Bhd, Times Subang, Lot 46, Subang Hi-Tech Industrial Park, Batu Tiga, 40000 Shah Alam, Selangor Darul Ehsan, Malaysia

Marshall Cavendish is a trademark of Times Publishing Limited

All websites were available and accurate when this book was sent to press.

Library of Congress Cataloging-in-Publication Data

Walker, Kate.
  Glass / Kate Walker.
    p. cm. — (Recycling)
  Includes index.
  Summary: "Discusses how glass is made and the variety of ways to recycle
it"—Provided by publisher.
  ISBN 978-1-60870-130-8
  1. Glass waste—Recycling—Juvenile literature. I. Title.
  TP859.7.W35 2011
  666'.14—dc22
                              2009041319

First published in 2009 by
MACMILLAN EDUCATION AUSTRALIAN PTY LTD
15–19 Claremont Street, South Yarra 3141

Visit our website at www.macmillan.com.au or go directly to www.macmillanlibrary.com.au

Associated companies and representatives throughout the world.

Edited by Julia Carlomagno
Text and cover design by Christine Deering
Page layout by Christine Deering
Photo research by Legend Images
Illustrations by Gaston Vanzet

Printed in the United States

Acknowledgments
The author and the publisher are grateful to the following for permission to reproduce copyright material:

Front cover photograph: Girl recycling glass bottles, photo by David Woodfall/Getty Images

Photos courtesy of: Coo-ee Picture Library, 8; Jaqueline Cooley, 26 top and bottom, 27; The DW Stock Picture Library, 30 top and bottom; EnviroGLAS, photo by Tim, 28 both; Gabriel M. Covian/Getty Images, 13 left; Monty Rakusen/Getty Images, 9 right; Russell Sadur/Getty Images, 22; Stockbyte/ Getty Images, 14; Frank Scherschel/Time & Life Pictures/Getty Images, 9 center; Pete Turner/Getty Images, 7 right; David Woodfall/Getty Images, 1; Glassco.ie, 12 center; © Robert Byron/iStockphoto, 17; © Alexander Kalina/iStockphoto, 18 left; © Sava Miokovic/iStockphoto, 21; © Ellen Poche/ iStockphoto, 12 right; © Ralph125/iStockphoto, 5; © Elzbieta Sekowska/iStockphoto, 3; © 2008 Jupiterimages, 6; © Peter E. Smith, Natural Sciences Image Library, 7 left, 12 left, 20 (photo produced with permission from Meta Processing Ltd., New Zealand); Photolibrary © Photo Network/Alamy, 29; Photolibrary/James L Amos, 13 right; Photolibrary/Sue Atkinson, 23; Photolibrary/Imagesource, 15; Photolibrary/Martin Bond/SPL, 4; Photolibrary/ Maximilian Stock Ltd/SPL, 9 left; © Milushkina Anastasiya/Shutterstock, 18 right; © Asther Lau Choon Siew/Shutterstock, 30 center; Visy Recycling, photo taken at Basin Primary School, reproduced with permission, 16.

While every care has been taken to trace and acknowledge copyright, the publisher tenders their apologies for any accidental infringement where copyright has proved untraceable. Where the attempt has been unsuccessful, the publisher welcomes information that would redress the situation.

Contents

Glossary Words

When a word is printed in **bold**, you can look up its meaning in the Glossary on page 31.

What Is Recycling?

Recycling is collecting used products and making them into new products. Recycling is easy and keeps the environment clean.

Every glass bottle that is recycled saves resources and helps the environment.

Why Recycle Glass?

Recycling glass helps:

- save **natural resources** for future use
- reduce **pollution** in the environment
- keep waste material out of **landfills**

If more glass was recycled, landfills such as this one could be closed.

Glass Products

People use many different glass products every day. Glass is used in:

- bottles
- food jars
- drinking glasses
- windows

Many different types of glass products are found in most homes.

Glass is also used in products that do not look like glass. Fiberglass and road-marking paint are two products made with glass.

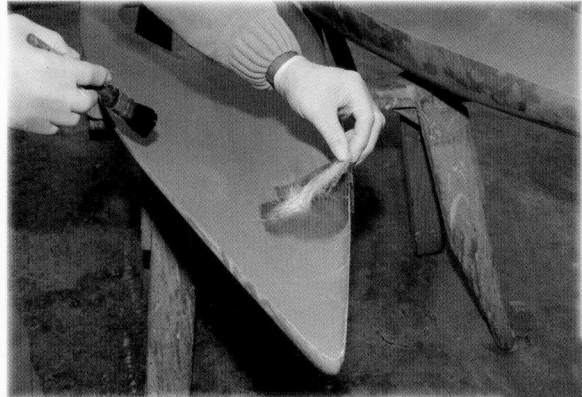

Fiberglass is a mixture of glass and plastic used to make boats and surfboards.

Road-marking paint contains tiny glass beads that reflect light from car headlights at night.

How Glass Is Made

Glass is made by heating sand until it melts and turns **transparent**. Sand is a natural resource with many uses. Cement is also made from sand.

The best sand for making glass is fine, white beach sand.

The Glass-Making Process

Sand goes through a three-stage **process** called **firing** to make glass.

Stage 1
Fine sand is mixed in a machine with chemicals to make it melt faster.

Stage 2
The mixed sand is fired inside a **furnace** until it melts.

Stage 3
Molten glass is taken out of the furnace and molded into glass products.

Throwing Away Glass or Recycling Glass?

Throwing away glass uses natural resources, increases pollution, and adds to waste.

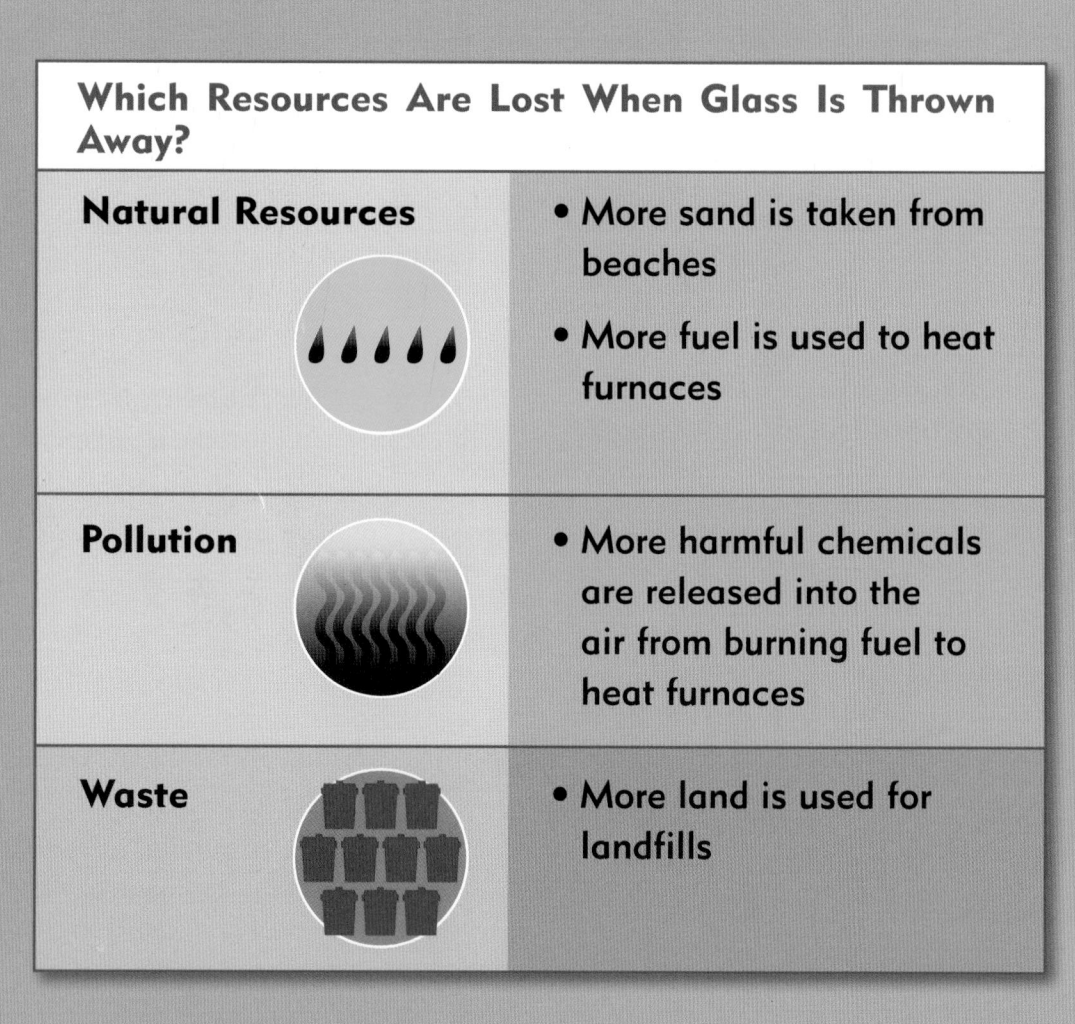

Which Resources Are Lost When Glass Is Thrown Away?

Natural Resources	• More sand is taken from beaches • More fuel is used to heat furnaces
Pollution	• More harmful chemicals are released into the air from burning fuel to heat furnaces
Waste	• More land is used for landfills

Recycling glass saves natural resources, reduces pollution, and cuts down on waste. Which do you think is better, throwing away or recycling glass?

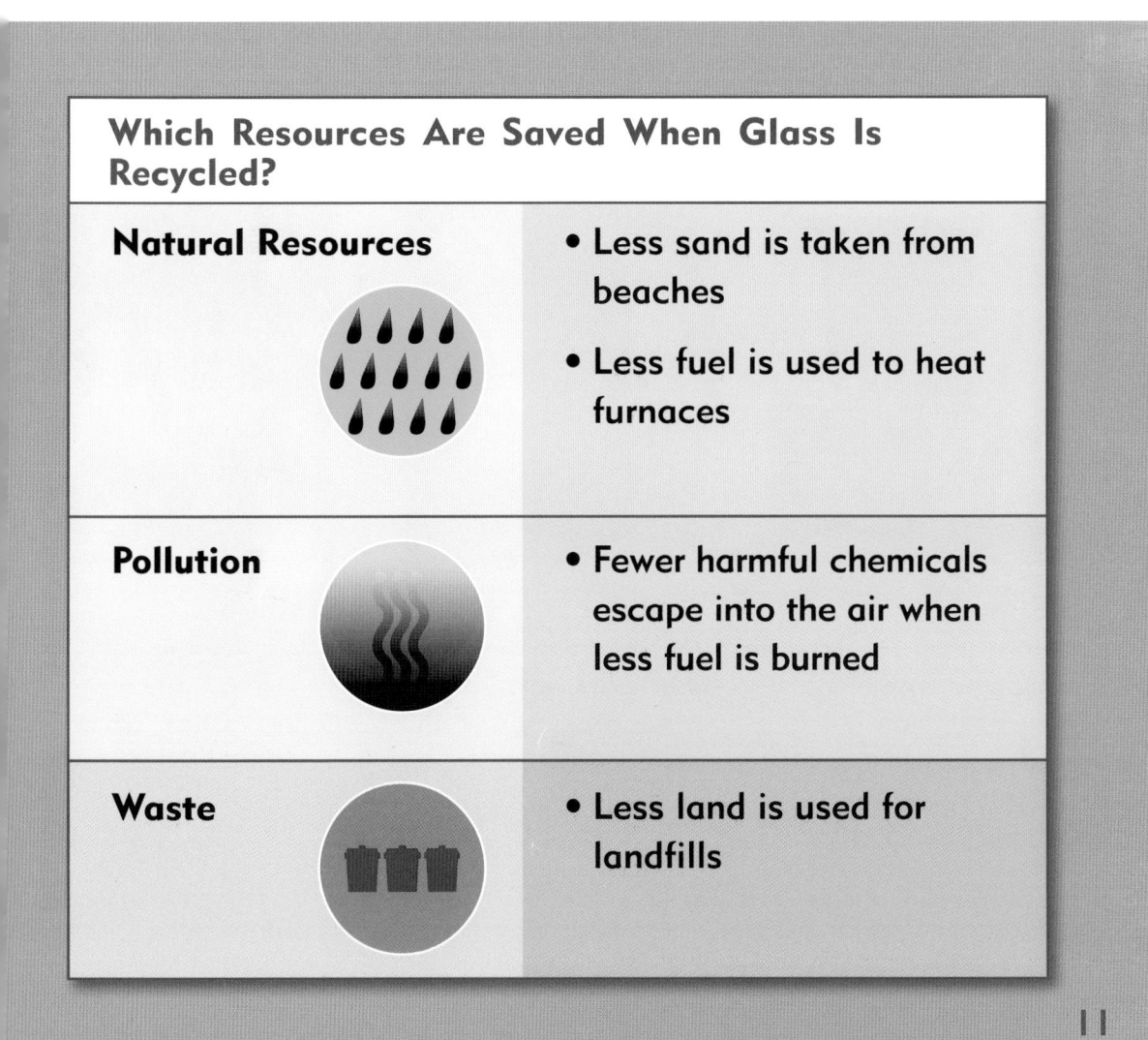

Which Resources Are Saved When Glass Is Recycled?

Natural Resources		• Less sand is taken from beaches • Less fuel is used to heat furnaces
Pollution		• Fewer harmful chemicals escape into the air when less fuel is burned
Waste		• Less land is used for landfills

How Glass Is Recycled

Glass is recycled through a five-stage process. This process begins when we recycle used glass. It ends with new glass products.

Stage 1
Used glass is collected from recycling bins left at the curb.

Stage 2
Glass is separated into **pure streams** of clear, green, and brown glass.

Stage 3
Glass is crushed into small pieces called **cullet**. Cullet is washed to remove labels and food.

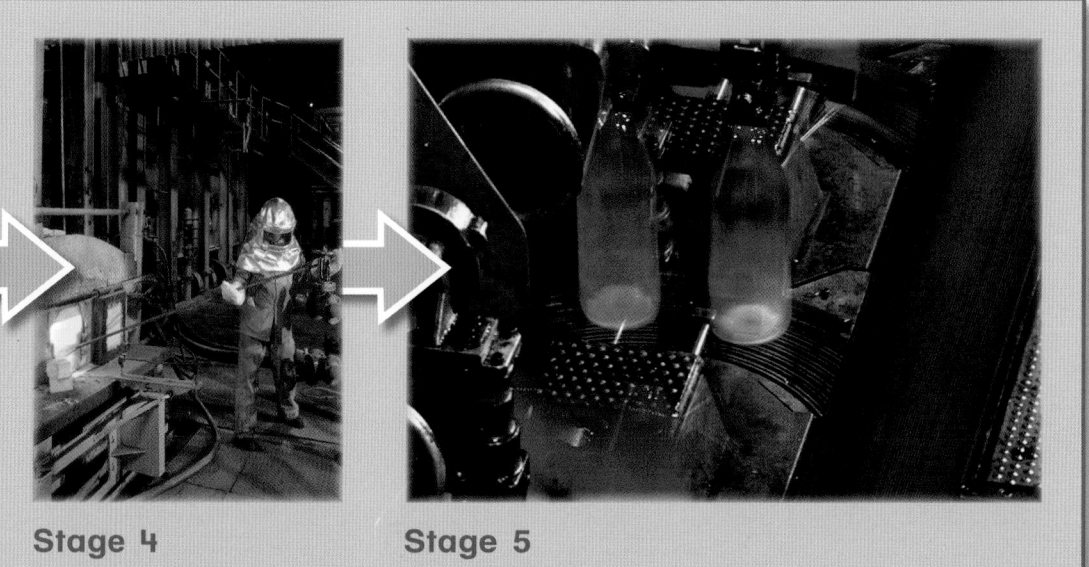

Stage 4
Cullet is fired in a furnace with new sand.

Stage 5
Molten glass is made into new glass products.

Recycling Glass at Home

Most households in towns and cities have special recycling bins. All **recyclable** glass can be put into these bins.

Glass is put into recycling bins, so it can be collected by recycling trucks.

How to Recycle Glass

The correct way to recycle glass is:
- remove metal and plastic lids
- wash glass containers in water
- keep plastic bags out of recycling bins

Make sure that only glass goes into glass-recycling bins.

Recycling Glass at School

Glass is used at school for food jars and bottles. Some schools have a special bin for collecting used glass. A team of **monitors** looks after the bin.

Monitors check that no garbage has been tossed in the glass-recycling bin.

Bottle Banks

Some schools set up **bottle banks** on school grounds for the whole community to use. Bottle banks are large, sturdy containers in which glass can be stored safely.

Bottle banks have separate containers for clear, brown, and green glass.

Can All Glass Be Recycled?

Not all glass can be recycled. Clear, green, and brown glass are recyclable. All other types of glass have chemicals in them that make them **nonrecyclable**.

Lightbulbs and blue glass are nonrecyclable.

Broken glass should not be recycled. Sorters at recycling centers can be harmed by broken glass.

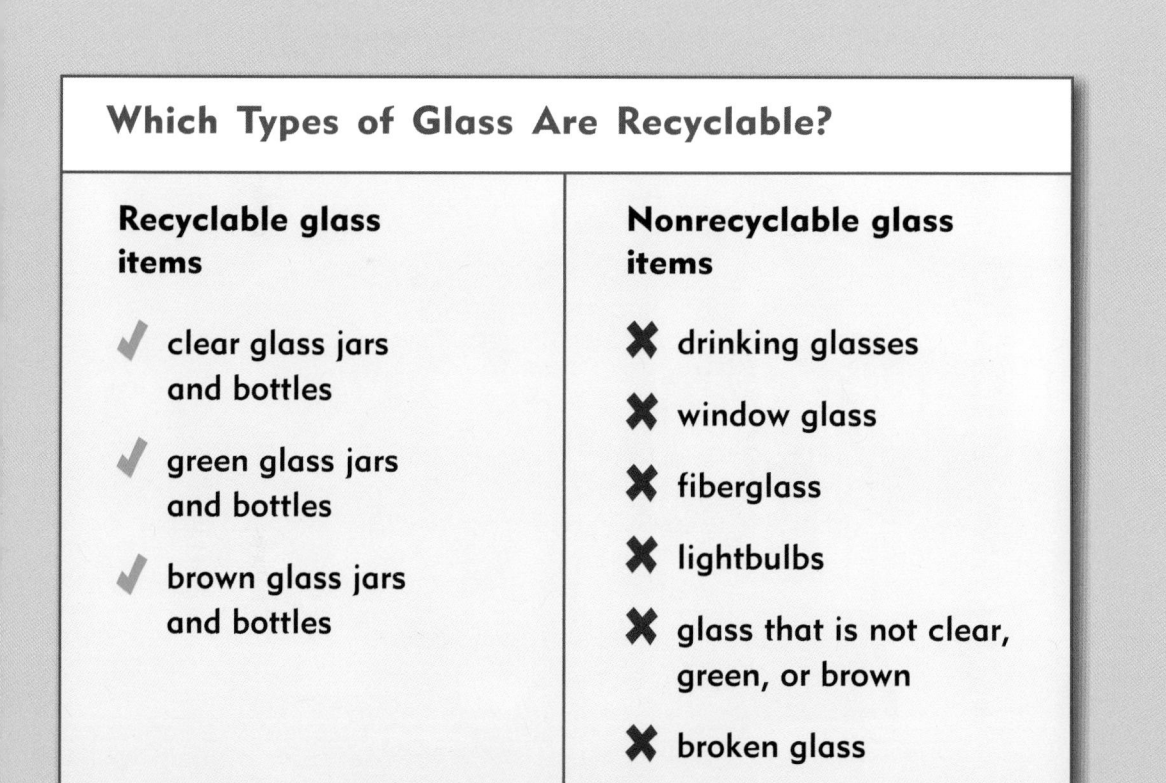

Which Types of Glass Are Recyclable?

Recyclable glass items	Nonrecyclable glass items
✓ clear glass jars and bottles	✗ drinking glasses
✓ green glass jars and bottles	✗ window glass
✓ brown glass jars and bottles	✗ fiberglass
	✗ lightbulbs
	✗ glass that is not clear, green, or brown
	✗ broken glass

Is Recycling Glass the Best Option?

Recycling glass saves fuel and helps the environment. However, recycling glass uses resources. **Electricity** is needed to crush glass and turn it into cullet.

This grinder uses electricity to crush glass into cullet.

Glass is very heavy to transport. Trucks that collect glass for recycling burn **fossil fuels** in their engines. Burning fossil fuels causes air pollution.

Trucks that carry glass to be recycled burn fossil fuels, which causes air pollution.

Reducing and Reusing Glass

There are many ways to reuse glass and to reduce the need for new glass. One way is to use the same glass containers many times.

Glass jars make great containers for paper clips.

Some simple ways to reuse glass are:

- save glass jars to use as flower vases
- donate glass jars with lids to charities and school art departments
- make jams or sauces and store them in glass jars

Homemade jam can be stored in recycled glass jars.

Make a Glass-Bottle Xylophone

A xylophone is a musical instrument that you strike to make different musical notes. Make a xylophone from recycled glass bottles.

What You Will Need:
- several empty glass bottles
- two metal spoons
- a pitcher filled halfway with water
- a funnel

What to Do:

1. Line up the empty glass bottles on the table.

2. Pour water from the jug into the first bottle until it is two-thirds full.

3. Pour water into the other
   bottles, adding less water
   each time.

4. Tap the bottles lightly with the
   spoons. Make a tune from the
   different musical notes.

School Recycling Projects

Students from schools in Newcastle-Under-Lyme in the United Kingdom helped to create a stained-glass window. The window was made from recycled car windshields and used glass bottles.

Students made molds, including some shaped like local buildings.

The molds were filled with recycled glass cullet.

Glass artist Jaqueline Cooley helped students to design and prepare the molds. The glass was fired in a small furnace called a kiln. The sections were put together with a metal frame.

Glass artist Jaqueline Cooley shows the stained-glass window.

Recycling Glass

Carolyn G. Bukhair Elementary School in Dallas, Texas, has special floors. They are made of used glass.

These shining school floors are made of used glass bottles and jars.

The floors were laid by a local glass recycler called EnviroGLAS. Seeing the glass floors has encouraged students to become recyclers, too.

Some students recycle paper, plastic, and glass at the end of each day.

How Recycling Glass Helps Animals

Glass is made from sand. Taking sand from beaches destroys animal **habitats**. When you recycle glass you save the habitats of many animals, including:

- soldier crabs

- terns

- turtles

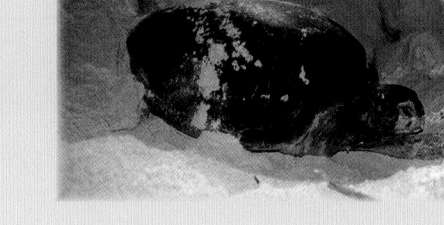

Glossary

bottle banks	Large bins that hold glass for recycling.
cullet	Glass crushed for recycling.
electricity	A type of power often used to run machines.
firing	A process in which sand is heated until it melts.
fossil fuels	Oil-based fuels that power engines in cars and trucks.
furnace	A machine used to heat and melt materials.
habitats	Areas where animals live, feed, and breed.
landfills	Large holes in the ground where waste material is buried.
molten	Changed into liquid by extreme heat.
monitors	Students who are given special duties.
natural resources	Materials found in nature that people use and value.
nonrecyclable	Not able to be recycled.
pollution	Waste that damages the air, water, or land.
process	A series of actions that brings about a change.
pure streams	Groups of items made of the same material.
recyclable	Able to be recycled.
transparent	See-through.

Index